The Common Cold

by Beth Bence Reinke

PEBBLE
a capstone imprint

Pebble Explore is published by Pebble, an imprint of Capstone.
1710 Roe Crest Drive
North Mankato, Minnesota 56003
www.capstonepub.com

Copyright © 2022 by Capstone. All rights reserved. No part of
this publication may be reproduced in whole or in part, or stored
in a retrieval system, or transmitted in any form or by any means,
electronic, mechanical, photocopying, recording, or otherwise,
without written permission of the publisher.

**Library of Congress Cataloging-in-Publication Data is available on
the Library of Congress website.**
ISBN: 978-1-6639-0819-3 (hardcover)
ISBN: 978-1-6639-2103-1 (paperback)
ISBN: 978-1-6639-0816-2 (eBook PDF)

Summary: The common cold causes sniffles and sneezes across the
globe each year. Although the virus that causes this annoying illness
spreads easily, there are things we can do to prevent it. Expertly
leveled text and vibrant photos help readers learn how to recognize
and prevent the common cold.

Image Credits
Shutterstock: A3pfamily, 12, 23, Andrey_Popov, 5, Andrii
Medvednikov, 19, BlurryMe, 15, Chanintorn.v, Cover, Daisy Daisy, 27,
Dawn Shearer, 9, JPC-PROD, 17, Juriah Mosin, 21, LightField Studios,
11, photonova, design element, Prostock-studio, 29, Stephanie Frey,
25, Tom Wang, 7

Editorial Credits
Editor: Gena Chester; Designer: Kazuko Collins; Media Researcher:
Jo Miller; Production Specialist: Tori Abraham

All internet sites appearing in back matter were available and
accurate when this book was sent to press.

Printed and bound in China. 4205

Table of Contents

Words in **bold** are in the glossary.

What Is the Common Cold?

Everyone gets a cold sometimes. A cold is the most common illness. That's why it is called the common cold.

A cold is an infection in the body's **airways**. Colds start in the nasal passages and throat.

A tiny germ called a **virus** causes a cold. There are more than 200 different cold viruses. Many are called **rhinoviruses**.

Anyone can get the common cold. But kids get more colds than adults. Some kids get up to eight colds a year.

Cold viruses are always around. You can catch a cold any time of year. But most people get colds in fall and winter. Cold viruses spread more easily in winter. It's cold outside. People are indoors together. One person has a cold. They can spread it to others.

When people are indoors in winter,
cold viruses can spread more easily.

How Cold Viruses Spread

Cold viruses are **contagious**. This means they spread from person to person. Say a friend has a cold. You spend time with your friend at school. Soon, you get a cold too.

But how did the virus infect you? The virus is in your friend's **mucus**. It's also in **saliva**. Your friend sneezes or coughs. Droplets fly out. Droplets might hit your eyes or mouth. You might breathe in droplets too.

Droplets can spread to things people touch. Sometimes the virus gets on toys. Other kids touch the toys. They touch their eyes, noses, or mouths. The virus infects their bodies.

Inside the body, the cold virus goes to work. It gets inside a healthy cell. The virus takes over. The cell makes copies of the virus. Soon there are many new copies. They make the person sick.

The cold virus can be in droplets that land on toys.

A sick person's body fights back. Extra mucus fills your nose. Mucus in the nose traps cold viruses. Usually, mucus is clear. But it may change color with a cold. It may turn green or yellow. That is normal. The color is caused by helper cells.

Helper cells are made in the body. These are called white blood cells. They fight the viruses. Some helper cells eat the cold viruses. Others make **antibodies**. Antibodies fight the viruses too.

Being Sick With a Cold

The common cold is a mild illness. **Symptoms** start slowly. At first, your throat feels scratchy. Then you sneeze. Achoo! Your nose gets stuffy. So you breathe through your mouth. Then your throat gets sore. You might also have a low fever.

A cold can make a person cough.

A cold makes you feel tired. Your eyes can feel heavy. They might be watery too. Mucus drips down your throat. It tickles. That makes you cough. You blow your nose a lot too. That helps get rid of the mucus.

A cold lasts about a week.
The cough can last a little longer.
So can the sniffles.

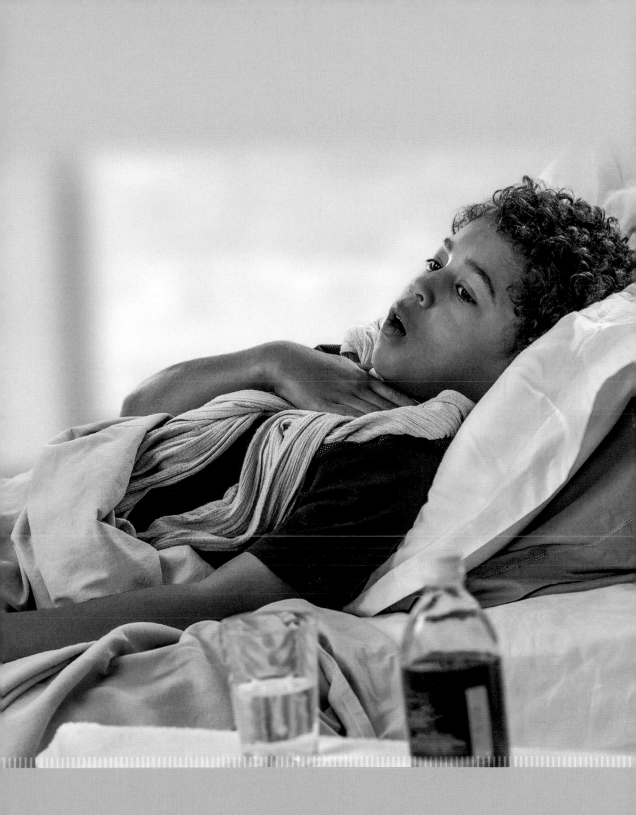

A cold can feel like other illnesses. One illness is called the flu. The cold and the flu cause coughs and stuffy noses. But different types of viruses cause the flu.

The flu can make you feel sick faster. Plus it has other symptoms. The flu can give you a high fever. It can cause body aches too. The flu is often worse than a cold.

A thermometer can be
used to check for a fever.

Treating a Cold

There is no cure for a cold. But there are ways to feel better. Get a lot of rest. Go to bed early. Take naps during the day.

Fluids also help your body fight the cold. Drink lots of water. Eat freeze pops. Cool fluids soothe your sore throat. Hot drinks help too. They help loosen mucus. That helps clear your stuffy nose. Sip tea with lemon. Eat chicken soup.

Medicines can't get rid of a cold.
But they might make you feel better.
A trusted adult can give you medicine.
Some medicines clear your nose.
Others help soothe your throat.

Most people stay home while they have a cold. They take good care of themselves. But sometimes a cold lasts too long. Infections can develop. An infection can cause a high fever. It can also cause breathing problems. Then it's time to see a doctor.

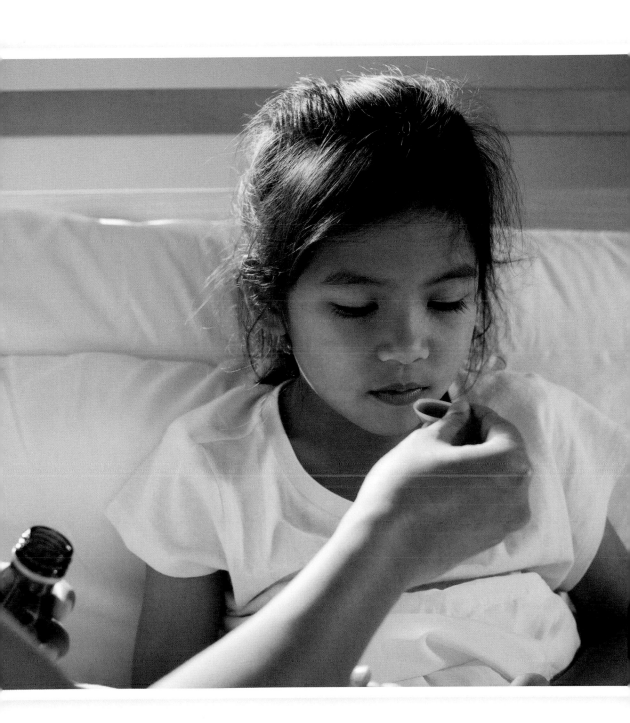

Preventing Colds

Vaccines help prevent the flu. People get flu shots each year. But there is no vaccine for the common cold.

There are ways to keep from spreading a cold. Stay home when you are sick. That helps protect others. Cough and sneeze into your elbow. Use a tissue when you can. Throw it in the trash. Wash your hands right away. Also, do not share cups or utensils.

Remember germs can get into your mouth, nose, and eyes. Be mindful after you touch something in public. Don't touch your mouth or nose. Don't rub your eyes.

Wash your hands often. This helps protect you from viruses. Use warm water. Rub the soap in your palms. Scrub between your fingers. Get the tops of your hands too. Then wash your fingernails.

Wash for 20 seconds. You can set a timer. Try counting to 20 slowly. You could sing the ABCs. Hum the "Happy Birthday" song twice.

Staying Healthy

Keep your body healthy to help fight cold viruses. Choose healthy foods. Eat fruits and vegetables. Drink enough water too. Get plenty of sleep. Kids need 10 hours every night. Your body heals while you sleep.

Move your body every day. Your body needs exercise to stay well. Ride your bike. Play tag or go for a walk.

Relax and have fun. Laughter is good for your health. You can help yourself stay well.

Drinking water can help you stay healthy.

Glossary

airway (ERH-way)—a breathing passage such as the nose, throat, and lungs

antibody (AN-tih-bah-dee)—a substance made by the body to fight germs

contagious (kun-TAY-jis)—spreads easily from person to person

mucus (MYOO-kiss)—liquid made by cells inside the nose and breathing passages

rhinovirus (RY-noh-vy-rus)—a kind of virus that causes colds

saliva (suh-LY-vuh)—fluid that keeps the mouth moist

symptom (SIMP-tum)—a sign the body shows when it is sick

vaccine (vak-SEEN)—a substance that helps the body protect itself from a specific illness

virus (VY-rus)—a tiny germ that can make people sick

Read More

Borgert-Spaniol, Megan. *Taking on Colds*. ABDO, 2020.

Tolosa Sistere, Moriona. *The Secret Life of Viruses: Incredible Science Facts about Germs, Vaccines, and What You Can Do to Stay Healthy*. Naperville: Sourcebooks Explore, 2021.

Tolosa Sistere, Moriona. *The Secret Life of Boogers: All the Amazing Facts that Make Your Snot Spectacular*. Naperville: Sourcebooks Explore, 2020.

Internet Sites

KidsHealth: Colds
kidshealth.org/en/kids/colds.html

KidsHealth: Why Does My Nose Run?
kidshealth.org/en/kids/nose-run.html?

KidsHealth: Why Do I Need to Wash My Hands?
kidshealth.org/en/kids/wash-hands.html?

Index